# A Cat for Keeps

June Crebbin

Illustrated by Peter Kavanagh

Tom Bates
10 Elmfield Avenue
Cambridge
CB2 5RS

CAMBRIDGE
UNIVERSITY PRESS

"I wish I had a cat," said Tom, after breakfast.

Grandma's fat tabby cat was staying with them for the weekend. Tom picked her up and stroked her fur. It was so warm and soft.

"We often *do* have a cat," said Mum. "Every time Grandma goes away."

"I mean for keeps," said Tom. "I wish I had a cat for keeps."

"I know you do," said Mum.

The postman arrived with a letter. It was for Tom.
"Let *me* see," said Emma.
"No," said Mum. "It's for Tom!"

It's for Tom!

Tom was surprised. It wasn't his birthday. He opened
the envelope carefully. Inside was a letter and four tickets.
"Who's it from?" said Emma.

Tom looked at the bottom of the letter. "It's from
Uncle Jack," he said.

Uncle Jack wasn't a real uncle, but he was Mum and Dad's
best friend and Tom's godfather. He was an actor.

"What does it say?" said Emma. Mum helped Tom read
the letter.

17 Abbey Street
London
SE7 7HG
15th December

Dear Tom,

How are you? I am in London at the moment, in a pantomime. This year I'm the cat in 'Dick Whittington' and I'm called Tommy!

Here are four tickets for the show. I hope you can come. They're for the last performance, so it should be a special one. Don't forget to come back stage after the show.

Love to your Mum, Dad, Ben and Emma.

Lots of love,
Uncle Jack.

Grand Theatre
Dick Whittington
JANUARY 21st
STALLS A 7 ∗ EVENING

"Isn't that kind?" said Mum.

Emma picked up the tickets. "But there are only four tickets," she said, "and there are five of us."

Mum explained that Ben was too little to go all the way to London to see a show. He would stay with Grandma.

Dad came in with the shopping. He wanted to hear all about Tom's letter.

"Uncle Jack's the Cat," said Tom. "I can't wait to see him."

When the day of the show arrived, Ben went off happily to Grandma's. In the afternoon, Mum suggested that Tom and Emma should have a sleep. They would be out very late that night, later than Tom had ever been out before.

Tom tried to sleep but he felt too excited. He wondered if Uncle Jack would be a tabby cat or a black cat. Tom liked black cats best.

At last they set off for the station. Tom loved going on trains. At first, he enjoyed looking out of the window. He watched fields and trees flying by. He saw cows and sheep.

Then it became too dark to see anything. They had some sandwiches and drinks and they played some card games.

In London, Dad said, "Keep close to me. I don't want to lose you."

Tom didn't want to be lost. Crowds filled the streets. All around him people were jostling each other and bumping into him. Tom kept tight hold of Dad's hand.

Bright lights shone down from streetlights and out from cafés.
Cars and taxis passed by. Tom wanted to stop and watch.
But Dad was striding on and Tom skipped to keep up.

In the theatre, there was plenty of time for Tom to look around.
On the walls in the entrance hall there were some photos.
"Look," said Mum. "Here's a photo of Uncle Jack."
Tom looked. He saw a big brown cat with white whiskers.
"He looks just like a real cat," said Tom.

Captain Fitzwarren

Tommy the Cat

Sultan Suleiman

Their seats were right at the front. Thick curtains hid the stage, but Tom could see light underneath and things being moved about.

"They're getting ready," said Dad. "It won't be long now."

Tom looked at the programme. There was a photo of Uncle Jack in it. Underneath the photo it said: 'Tommy the Cat'.

"When will it start?" said Tom.

"Any minute now," said Dad. "And you never know, you might get a chance to join in."

"What do you mean?" said Tom, but at that moment the lights dimmed and the show began.

Tom watched for Tommy the Cat to come onto the stage.

Suddenly he was there – and what a cat! He purred and sprang. He danced and climbed. He even climbed the mast of a ship! Everyone loved him.

There was singing and dancing and then, after the interval, there was a song for the audience to sing. Children were invited to go on the stage. Some of the actors came down to fetch them.

Emma was out of her seat in a moment, but Tom felt too shy. Then Tommy the Cat came right up to him and took his hand.

"You'll be all right with me," he whispered.

All the children on the stage were given a balloon for singing so well. Tom went back to his seat in a daze.

"Well done," said Mum.

"Told you," said Dad.

At the end of the show, Tom clapped until his hands were stinging. Flowers were given to the leading actors. Tommy the Cat had a huge bunch of flowers. Then the curtains came down and it was time to go.

Uncle Jack was waiting for them in his dressing-room. He looked more like himself now. He had changed out of his costume, but he still had his make-up on.

Everyone talked excitedly, except Tom. He didn't know what to say. Uncle Jack smiled.

"I like your whiskers," said Tom.

"Would you like some?" said Uncle Jack. He sat Tom in
a chair. "How about a little black nose as well?"

"There," he said, when he had finished painting Tom's face.
"You're a Tom-cat now!"

Everyone laughed.

"Do you have a cat?" said Tom. "A cat of your own?"

"Yes, I do," said Uncle Jack. "Well, sort of."

He explained that he had found a stray kitten outside the theatre late one night. "She was so thin and weak," he said. "She was lucky to be alive. I've been feeding her and trying to find her a proper home. The show closes tonight. I'm going abroad, so I can't take her with me."

"I'd like a cat," said Tom. "Where is she?"

"That's just it," said Uncle Jack. "She went missing this morning. I can't find her anywhere."

Dad looked at his watch and said they really ought to be going. Uncle Jack came to the stage door with them and they all said goodbye.

"If you *should* see a kitten . . . ," said Uncle Jack, looking up and down the street. "She's completely black and she's wearing a red collar."

There wasn't much chance of seeing anything, Tom thought as they set off, because Dad was in a hurry again.

"Down here," said Dad, turning into a side-street. "I know a short-cut."

The street they turned into was narrow. Bright lights and noise were behind them and ahead of them, but in this street it was dark and quiet. Against one wall was a row of dustbins, some overflowing with rubbish. Tom hurried along behind Dad. Mum and Emma followed close behind.

Just as they came to the end of the street, Tom heard something.

"Stop!" said Tom.

"What for?" said Dad, turning into a brightly lit street.

"I heard something," said Tom. He tugged at Dad's hand. "I'm sure I heard a kitten."

"You can't hear anything with all this traffic," said Dad.

"Not here," said Tom, "back there. Please stop."
But Dad hurried on.

Tom tugged his hand loose.

He turned and ran back through the crowds. Behind him he heard Dad's angry voice shouting, and then he was in the quiet of the side-street.

He stood still and listened. At first, all he could hear was the traffic behind him. Then he heard the sound he had heard before. It sounded like a kitten crying. He moved towards the dustbins. There it was again – louder now. In front of him was a dustbin. Tom pulled the lid off.

Inside the dustbin was a tiny kitten. Tom lifted it out and stroked its fur. "It's all right," he whispered. "You're all right now."

It's all right. You're all right now.

Then Mum, Dad and Emma arrived. Dad was very angry with Tom, and at first he wouldn't let Tom take the kitten to Uncle Jack.

"We don't even know if this is his kitten," he said. "And we'll miss our train."

"She *is* completely black and she *does* have a red collar," said Emma.

"And there *is* another train," said Mum.

Tom held the kitten close.

"We can't leave her here," said Mum.

So they all went back to the theatre.

Uncle Jack couldn't believe his eyes when they all walked
in, with Tom carrying the kitten.

"But what will happen to her?" said Tom, still holding
her close.

"I don't know," said Uncle Jack. "I don't suppose . . . "
Tom looked at Dad, and then at Mum.

"She is rather sweet," said Mum.

"Please," said Tom. Dad looked at them. "We'll need a box
to carry her home in," he said.

When at last they were on the train, Tom said, "Thanks, Dad. Thanks, Mum."

Mum looked at Tom's face with its make-up still on – the little black nose and whiskers. "Trust one stray kitten to find another," she said.

GRAND THEATRE
SHAFTESBURY AVE.

Assorted Turkish Beards

"But," said Dad, "*never* go off like that again. We could have lost you."

"I won't," said Tom.

He sat back in his seat. Then he thought of something.

"I forgot to ask Uncle Jack what the kitten's name is."

"It's on her collar," said Mum. She lifted the kitten out of the box to show Tom.

'LUCKY,' it said. Tom settled the kitten on his lap. "So you're Lucky," he said.

"And so are you!" said Mum.

"Yes," said Tom. He stroked the kitten gently. "So am I."